# Amazing Animal
# Super - Sleuths

by Leon Gray

Raintree is an imprint of Capstone Global Library Limited, a company incorporated in England and Wales having its registered office at 7 Pilgrim Street, London EC4V 6LB Registered company number 6695582

**www.raintree.co.uk**
myorders@raintree.co.uk

ISBN: 978-1-4747-0217-1 (HB)
ISBN: 978-1-4747-0223-2

**For Brown Bear Books Ltd:**
Text: Leon Gray
Editor: Tim Harris
Picture Researcher: Clare Newman
Designer: Karen Perry
Design Manager: Keith Davis
Production Director: Alastair Gourlay
Editorial Director: Lindsey Lowe
Children's Publisher: Anne O'Daly

**British Library Cataloguing in Publication Data**
A full catalogue record for this book is available from the British Library.

**Acknowledgements**
Front cover: Elsa Hoffman/Shutterstock
1, Stuart G Porter/Shutterstock; 4, Ammit Jack/Shutterstock; 5tr, Theo Klein/Thinkstock; 5bl, pwrmc/Shutterstock; 5bc, Stephen Fink/Getty Images; 6b, Michal Ninger/Shutterstock; 6-7, Maggy Meyer/Shutterstock; 7tr, Stuart G Porter/Shutterstock; 8, Justin Black/Shutterstock; 9tr, The Print Collector/Alamy; 9b, Bryan Buscovicki/Shutterstock; 10cl, Andrew M. Allport/Shutterstock; 10cr, Mariusz Szczygiel/Shutterstock; 11t, Igor Kovalenko/Shutterstock; 11br, Michal Ninger/Shutterstock; 12, Ivan Kuzmin/Shutterstock; 13t, Ehtesham/Shutterstock; 13b, Mark Medcalf/Shutterstock; 15t, Ivan Kuzmin/Shutterstock; 15b, NOAA; 16, Iakov Filimonov/Dreamstime; 17t, Lenar Musin/Shutterstock; 17b, Dickie Duckett/FLPA; 18, F1online/FLPA; 18-19, Bildagentur Zoonar GmbH/Shutterstock; 19tr, Vanessa Grossemy/Alamy; 20, Bimka/Shutterstock; 21tr, Monika Wisniewska/Shutterstock; 21b, Michael Cummings/Getty Images; 22, Mike Parry/Minden Pictures/FLPA; 23tr, Stephen Fink/Getty Images; 23b, Frantisekhojdysz/Shutterstock; 24, Tom Wang/Shutterstock; 24-25, Cbenjasuwan/Shutterstock; 25t, Wacpan/Shutterstock; 26, Tomatillo/Shutterstock; 27tr, Kurcharski K. Kucharska/Shutterstock; 27b, Bo. Valentino/Shutterstock; 29t, Kim Jae-Hwan/AFP/Getty Images; 29b, Marjan Visser Photography/Shutterstock.
t=top, c=centre, b=bottom, l=left, r=right

All artworks © Brown Bear Books Ltd
Brown Bear Books has made every attempt to contact the copyright holder.
If anyone has any information please contact licensing@brownbearbooks.co.uk

Some words are shown in bold, **like this**. You can find out what they mean by looking at the glossary.

Printed in China
20  19  18  17  16
10  9 8 7 6 5 4 3 2 1

# Contents

# Introduction

**Animals depend on their senses for survival. They use their senses to avoid danger and to find and catch prey. Animals also need their senses to find mates.**

Many animals have the same five senses that humans have – sight, smell, sound, taste and touch. Often, their senses are sharper than our own. Hunters, such as big cats and birds of prey, have excellent eyesight. Bats, owls and other creatures that hunt at night need super hearing. Dogs use their sense of smell to follow trails of scent.

Other animals have developed special senses that people do not have. Fish, crabs, spiders, bees, butterflies and snakes, for example, can detect things such as movement and warmth in ways that people cannot.

Read on to find out about animals with the clearest vision, the sharpest hearing and the most unusual ways of sensing the world around them.

## Inspired by nature

Humans have copied some of these amazing senses. **Sonar** maps the floor of the ocean. It is based on the same techniques used by bats and dolphins when they are hunting. Satellite dishes focus signals in much the same way as owls focus sound with their **facial discs**. Some dogs are so good at following scent that people use them to hunt for criminals and to search for dangerous things such as explosives.

## COPYCAT

The facial disk of an owl funnels s ... ... ... ... ears in ... way as a ... TV sign... receive...

## WOW

Scientists have found that sharks can smell a single drop of blood in one million drops of water. Sharks rely on their incredible sense of smell to track down prey from hundreds of metres away.

## Guide for readers

Throughout this book, special feature boxes accompany the main text, captioned photographs and illustrations. COPYCAT boxes highlight some of the ways in which people have been inspired by the animal world. WOW boxes provide incredible facts and figures about the different animals.

# Super sight

Many animals have much better eyesight than people have. They can see further and more clearly. Some animals can even see things that are invisible to our own eyes.

## Predators and prey

Almost all animals have eyes. Predators (animals that hunt other animals) have eyes on the front of their head. These forward-facing eyes work together to focus on objects such as the animal's next meal. Big cats, including lions and tigers, dogs, bears and birds of prey, are all examples of predatory animals. Many **prey** animals, such as rabbits and mice, have eyes on each side of their head. These animals use one eye to look for food and the other eye to keep watch for danger.

## Seeing the light

An animal sees the light that reflects off objects around it. Its eyes focus the light onto a thin layer at the back of each eye. This layer is called the retina. It is very sensitive to light and converts it into signals that go to the animal's brain. Some **receptors** in the retina are sensitive to different colours, while others are better at seeing in the dark. The brain turns all this information into a picture.

An owl has large eyes and very sharp vision. It can see small things far away.

**BIRDS OF PREY CASE STUDY: PAGE 10**

Lions have very good eyesight. They can see clearly by day and at night.

This cheetah is sprinting after a young gazelle on a grassland in Africa.

**CHEETAHS**
**CASE STUDY: PAGE 8**

# Cheetahs

Cheetahs are top predators that rely on their super sense of sight – and their amazing speed – to catch prey such as gazelles and zebras.

A cheetah has black lines, called "tear lines", between each eye and its mouth.

## Built for speed

Cheetahs are big cats. They are the slender, spotted relatives of lions and tigers. Most cheetahs hunt on the scorching grasslands of southern Africa, although a few live in Iran. Cheetahs are the world's fastest land animals. They can sprint at an incredible 120 kilometres per hour (75 mph). However, when they are hunting, speed is not enough. These predators need to see prey when it is far away – and to be able to judge distances correctly. Cheetahs have eyes that do both.

## Amazing vision

Unlike most big cats, cheetahs hunt during the day. They often sit on a fallen tree or rocky ledge, scanning the horizon for their next meal. They rely on binocular vision. That means that both eyes work together to give the cheetah a sharp, wide-angle view of its surroundings. A cheetah has eyesight sharp enough to spot prey 8 kilometres (5 miles) away.

Cheetahs have distinctive black marks, called "tear lines", running from each eye to the mouth. Scientists believe that these marks reduce the glare of the sun. This helps the cheetah see clearly even on the brightest days.

# WOW

The ancient Egyptians often tamed wild cheetahs and kept them as hunting companions. During the hunt, a cheetah would be kept on a leash, with its head covered by a hood. When the hunters spotted another animal they removed the hood. The cheetah chased and killed the prey.

This cheetah is scanning the African grassland for its next meal.

# Birds of prey

For a bird, vision is the most important sense of all. Birds rely on good eyesight to fly safely, and birds of prey need sharp eyes to spot their prey.

A hawk soars high as it looks for prey. It has a clear view of the ground (below).

## Large eyes

Birds of prey have an amazing sense of sight. They have large eyes that allow larger images to be shown on the retina at the back of each eye. The point of sharpest vision on the retina is called the fovea. People have one fovea in each eye, but birds of prey have two. Each fovea is packed with light-sensitive cells called cones. The bird's brain turns the information from cones into a sharp colour image.

Bald eagles can see fish swimming beneath the surface of rivers and lakes.

# WOW

Birds have some of the largest eyes relative to their body size in the animal kingdom. If our own eyes were in the same proportion as those of an eagle, they would be as big as oranges.

Hawks, eagles and falcons are birds of prey. They all have millions of cones in each eye. Birds of prey have spectacular long-distance vision. An eagle can see a rabbit 3.2 kilometres (2 miles) away.

Some birds of prey can see things people cannot. Kestrels have special cone cells that pick up **ultraviolet** light. This helps the kestrels find voles and mice, their favourite food. Voles and mice are difficult to see. They run around in thick grass. However, kestrels can see the trails of urine that voles leave behind. The trails reflect ultraviolet light.

# Sharp ears

Some animals have incredibly sharp hearing. They can detect even sounds that people and some animals cannot hear.

## Waves of sound

Sounds are tiny **vibrations** that travel in waves. When someone speaks, his or her **vocal cords** vibrate. The vibrations make air particles in their mouth bump into each other. The particles bump into others close by, starting sound waves. People who are nearby will hear the voice of the person who is speaking.

## Ears to hear

All **vertebrates** have ears. Some animals have **external** ears, which funnel sounds into the inner ear, inside the head. Tiny hairs line the walls of the inner ear. The hairs turn the vibrations of the sound waves into **nerve** signals. The brain understands these signals as sound.

Some animals can hear a much wider range of sounds than humans. Whales can hear sounds with a low **pitch**. Bats can hear sounds with a very high pitch, called **ultrasound**.

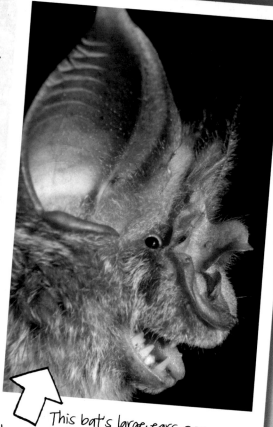

This bat's large ears can hear sounds that people cannot.

**BATS**
**CASE STUDY: PAGE 14**

The ears of owls are hidden away beneath feathers. The tufts on top of this owl's head are not real ears.

**OWLS**
**CASE STUDY: PAGE 16**

A jackrabbit has two long ears. These help it hear the sounds of hunting predators.

# Bats

Bats are small flying mammals that rely on a supersonic sense of hearing to "see" in sound. This amazing ability helps bats to fly safely in the dark and locate moths and other food.

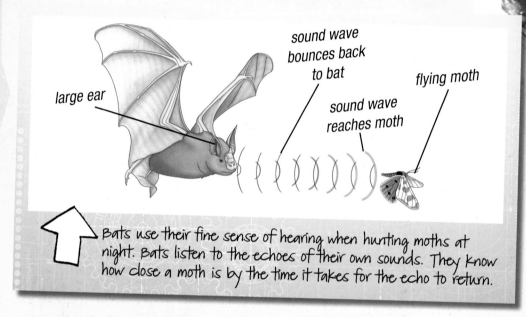

large ear

sound wave bounces back to bat

sound wave reaches moth

flying moth

Bats use their fine sense of hearing when hunting moths at night. Bats listen to the echoes of their own sounds. They know how close a moth is by the time it takes for the echo to return.

## Hunters in the dark

During the day, bats sleep in sheltered spaces. At night, they come out to feed on insects. Bats have fairly good eyesight, but this is not much use to them in the dark. Instead, they have another way of finding their way around—**echolocation**. This is a way of using sound to see. Bats make shouting sounds as they fly. The noise travels as a series of sound waves. These waves travel through the air until they hit a tree, a wall, or an insect. The waves bounce off the obstacle, and the bat hears the reflected sound as an echo.

Bats can fly in dark caves using echolocation.

## COPYCAT

People have created their own echolocation to explore the depths of the ocean. The system is called sonar. It sends sound into the water from remote-controlled submarines. Equipment listens for echoes from objects such as shipwrecks.

The sounds that bats make are very high-pitched. Most people cannot hear them. However, the sounds behave in the same way as any other sound, traveling through the air in waves and bouncing off objects in their path.

A bat's sense of hearing is extremely sensitive. When the bat hears an echo, it can figure out how big an object is and if it is moving. The bat's brain builds up an image of the world around it. This keeps the animal from flying into things and helps it find its prey.

# Owls

**An owl has super-sensitive hearing. It listens for tiny movements in leaves or the undergrowth. Owls can even hear the sounds of small animals hidden under a layer of snow.**

## Hidden ears

An owl's ears are on the sides of its head, just behind the eyes. Some owls have small, round ear openings. Other owls have long slits. The openings are covered by feathers. Some owls have a distinctive facial disk. The disk helps to guide sounds into the bird's ears.

## Pinpointing prey

An owl can hear the movements of mice and other prey. The owl compares the sound that arrives in each ear opening. If the left ear detects the sound of the mouse before the right ear, the owl knows its prey is on its left. If the owl turns its head toward the noise, the sound waves arrive at the same time. The owl then knows the mouse is straight ahead.

Many owls have a flattish facial disk. This funnels sound to the birds' ears.

The ears of some owls are in slightly different positions on each side of the head. One ear is slightly higher than the other. This helps the owl figure out whether a sound is coming from above or below its face.

Once the owl knows where its prey is, it flies straight toward it. The owl does not make a sound when it flies—its wings cut smoothly through the air. It keeps its head facing toward the direction of the last sound it heard. If the prey moves at the last minute, the owl listens out for the movement and alters its flight path. Just before it strikes, the owl spreads its **talons** in front of its face. It grabs hold of its victim and kills it.

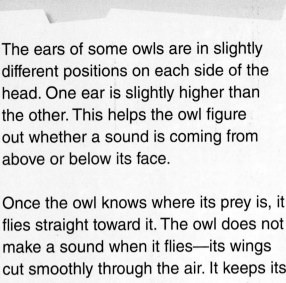

# COPYCAT

The facial disk of an owl funnels sounds into its ears in much the same way as a dish channels TV signals into the receiver on a house.

An owl flies off with a mouse it has just caught in its talons.

# Super sniffers

For many animals a sense of smell is vital. A keen sense of smell helps these animals track down food, pick up the scent of a mate or sniff a path through an unfamiliar place.

## Something in the air

The air is full of tiny scent chemicals called **molecules**. Animals use their sense of smell to detect these odours and work out what is making them.

When an animal sniffs the air, special receptor cells deep inside its nose pick up scent molecules. Different receptor cells are fine-tuned to smell different kinds of scent molecules. Scientists think that each molecule fits each receptor cell like a key fits a lock. The receptor cells feed the information to the brain.

Why do people think the **aroma** of ripe fruit or baking bread smells delicious, but the stench of rotten eggs smells unpleasant? It might be because it helps us avoid things that could harm us – rotting food is not good to eat. People do not have a good sense of smell compared with many animals. The best odour detectors include bears, sharks, dogs, rats and moths.

Scent molecules travel through water as well as air. This helps the shark find prey.

**SHARKS CASE STUDY: PAGE 22**

Bears sniff the air to pick up the scent of food, enemies or other bears.

A bloodhound can follow a trail of scent even when it is several days old.

DOGS AND WOLVES
CASE STUDY: PAGE 20

# Dogs and wolves

Smell is the most important sense for wild dogs such as wolves, coyotes and jackals. It is also important for pet dogs and dogs that have been trained to help people.

A dog's nose can smell food over long distances.

## Picking up the scent

The inside of a dog's nose has a spongy, moist **membrane**. This detects even the faintest odours wafting in the air. The membrane has hundreds of millions of smell receptors in it. It is so sensitive that a dog can pick up the scent of thousands of chemicals in the air. Nerves connect the smell receptors to the brain, so the animal can tell what it is sniffing. A dog's nose is much more sensitive to different odours than a person's nose.

## Sniffing for a meal

A wolf's sense of smell is up to 100 times more sensitive than our own. A wolf can smell the scent of a deer from 3.2 kilometres (2 miles) away if the wind is blowing from the direction of the prey.

Wolves live in social groups called packs. Members of a pack defend a **territory** from neighbouring groups. Every wolf in a pack marks the territory with scent. It releases the scent from **glands** near the base of its tail. The scent warns wolves from other packs to keep away.

## COPYCAT

Dogs have such a good sense of smell that dogs have trained them to help them. Sniffer dogs help police officers find illegal drugs and hidden explosives.

This wolf is sniffing the air to catch the scent of a distant animal to hunt.

# Sharks

A shark has an incredibly strong sense of smell. The shark's super-sensitive snout works with its other senses to make the animal a deadly predator.

nare

The small holes just above the shark's mouth are its sensitive nares.

## Super sense

A shark has one of the most sensitive noses of the animal kingdom. It has two openings called nares, one on each side of its snout. Each nare is made up of two tubes. The shark sucks seawater in through one of the tubes and snorts it out through the other. As the water travels through the shark's nose, it passes over a thin membrane. The membrane is packed with many scent receptors. These receptors send messages to the brain. The shark can quickly identify many different smells.

When the shark picks up the scent of food, it starts swimming towards it. As the shark speeds through the water, it detects more scent molecules (chemicals). By comparing the amount of scent in each nare, the shark knows which way to swim.

## Strange sense

As well as its amazing sense of smell, a shark can also hear and see well. And it has a special sense that people do not have. It can detect the tiny electrical **currents** made by other animals as they move. It does this by using receptors called the ampullae of Lorenzini. These receptors are tubes in the shark's head. They are filled with a jelly-like substance, which detects tiny movements.

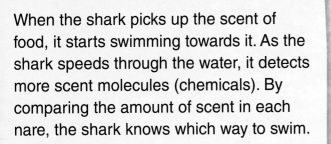

A shark can swim towards its prey quickly once it has picked up its scent.

# Special senses

Many animals have super-sensitive versions of our own senses of sight, touch, sound, smell and taste. Many more creatures have amazing special senses that are nothing like these.

## Feet that taste and hairs that hear

Over millions of years, some animals have developed other senses that help them survive. Butterflies and blowflies have receptor cells on their feet that allow these insects to "taste" what they are standing on. Scorpions and crabs have hairs on their pincers or claws that detect even the tiniest movements in water. Grasshoppers and spiders have hairs on their bodies that can pick up tiny air movements and the scent given off by other animals. Spiders also use these hairs to "hear" sounds.

Pit viper snakes know when there is a mouse or other prey close by – even when it is completely dark and the prey is not making a sound. The snake has a special organ that can "see" the warmth given off by the other animal. Fish have a unique "lateral line" sense, which tells them when another animal is coming close.

Bees and birds can sense changes in Earth's **magnetic field**. This sense helps them fly in the right direction when they are making long journeys.

Fish have a sensory system hidden away beneath their skin.

**FISH CASE STUDY: PAGE 28**

The hairs on a spider's legs help it sense what's going on around it.

SPIDERS CASE STUDY: PAGE 26

A butterfly has receptor cells in its six feet. The receptors let the insect know if a flower is good to feed on.

# Spiders

Scientists have identified about 44,000 different kinds of spiders. The spiders have several amazing senses that help them move around, find food and avoid their enemies.

Jumping spiders have eight eyes.

## Hairy legs

Some spiders have good eyesight. They see in much the same way as people see. Most spiders have eight eyes, not two. However, most spiders rely on other senses to find their way around and to catch their prey. One of the strangest of these is the way spiders hear sounds. Spiders use hundreds of fine hairs on their legs to listen for the movements of nearby insects. These hairs are called trichobothria.

A spider's hearing may seem odd, but it is not very different to the way that people hear sounds. The trichobothria on a spider's legs do the same job as the hairs inside human ears. The hairs pick up sound waves travelling through the air and convert them into electrical pulses that the spider's brain can understand.

## Taste and smell

Spiders have other sensory hairs on their legs. Some of these hairs are covered with tiny receptors that are sensitive to different chemicals. When a spider touches something with its legs, it actually tastes it. The same hairs pick up scent molecules in the air, so the spider uses its super-sensory legs to detect odours as well.

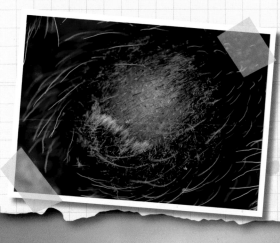

This tarantula spider can "hear" with the hundreds of hairs on its legs and body.

# Fish

Fish have an amazing sensory system that helps them detect the movements of other animals. It also helps them feel changes in their environment. This unique sense organ is called the lateral line system.

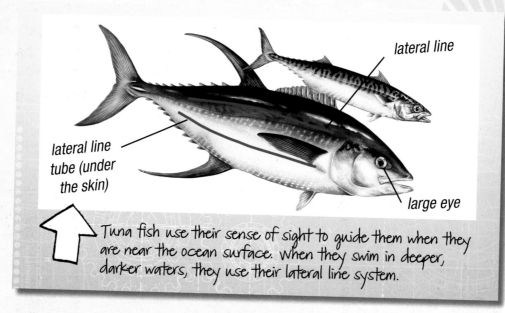

lateral line

lateral line tube (under the skin)

large eye

Tuna fish use their sense of sight to guide them when they are near the ocean surface. When they swim in deeper, darker waters, they use their lateral line system.

## Fish senses

Fish rely on a range of senses when they swim around in the ocean or fresh water. They have simple ears, but they cannot hear sounds very well. Instead, most fish use their strong sense of smell to detect food and avoid predators. They have good eyesight and can see different colours. Eyesight is not much use in deep water, because the Sun's rays cannot reach the depths of the ocean. In deep water, fish use a special sense called the lateral line system to help them make sense of their surroundings.

## COPYCAT

Scientists have built robots that use a similar device to the lateral line system of fish. These robots explore the ocean floor, looking for underwater caves and deep-sea volcanoes.

## Tubes and hairs

The lateral line is made up of a network of tubes that lie beneath the skin of a fish. Two long tubes run along each side of the fish's body, from the head to the end of its tail. Movements in the water pass through tiny **pores** in the fish's skin and into the lateral line system. As the water flows through the pores, it wafts fine hairs that lie along the walls of the tubes. When these hairs move, tiny electrical pulses are sent to the brain. In this way, the fish knows if a predator is swimming nearby. It also knows if the water **current** is changing direction.

These fishes' lateral line systems will warn them if a predator comes close.

# Glossary

**aroma**  scent or odour

**current**  movement of water in a river or the ocean

**external**  on the outside of an animal's body

**facial disc**  flattish area on the face of some birds of prey that directs sound to the ears

**glands**  organs that secrete substances into or out of an animal's body

**magnetic field**  area in which magnetic forces can be detected

**membrane**  thin layer of tissue, in a dog's nose, for example

**molecules**  tiny particles that are too small to see. Everything is made up of molecules.

**nerve**  fibre inside an animal's body that carries tiny pulses of electricity to and from the brain

**pitch**  how high or low a sound is

**pores**  tiny openings in the skin

**prey**  animal that is hunted and eaten by other animals

**receptors**  nerve endings that sense changes in light, warmth, sound, touch, smell or taste

**sonar**  technique using sound waves to detect the location, size and movement of underwater objects

**talons**  sharp claws on a bird of prey's foot

**territory**  area that is defended by a group of animals

**ultrasound**  type of sound where the sound waves travel very quickly

**ultraviolet**  light that some animals can detect, but which is invisible to the human eye

**vertebrates**  animals that have a backbone

**vibrations**  shaking movements

**vocal cords**  folds of skin in the throat that vibrate to produce sounds, such as your voice

# Read more

*Amazing Animal Senses* (Animal Superpowers), John Townsend (Raintree, 2013).

*Amazing Animal Senses* (Kingfisher Readers), Claire Llewellyn and Thea Feldman (Kingfisher, 2013).

*Cheetah* (Eye on the Wild), Suzi Eszterhas (Frances Lincoln, 2012).

*Eagles* (Amazing Animals), Sally Morgan (Franklin Watts, 2010).

*Nocturnal Animals* (100 Facts), Camilla de la Bedoyere (Miles Kelly, 2010).

*Super Natural: Animals,* Leon Gray (Wayland, 2013).

# Internet sites

**Neuroscience for Kids**
This site explains how different animals sense the world. faculty.washington.edu/chudler/amaze.html

**Science Photo Library**
An informative article on animal supersenses. www.sciencephoto.com/static/features/1180-Supersenses.pdf

**The Learning Zone**
Information on the different senses animals use, familiar and unusual. www.oum.ox.ac.uk/thezone/animals/life/sense.htm

# Index